I0157461

My Name is Desmond

A Collection of Stories about People who Share my Name

By Allison Dearstyne

For my brave and kindhearted Desmond Richard

The name Desmond came from Ireland. There was a kingdom there called Desmond from 1118 until 1596, so there was a whole kingdom that shared your name for hundreds of years! The Kingdom of Desmond was also called South Munster. At first, the name Desmond was a last name that meant you were from this kingdom, and later it became a first name. The name Desmond means "Gracious Defender." A defender bravely protects people.

The name Desmond has quite a history! Did you know that there have been heroes all around the world who share your name? We'll look at these seven men named Desmond in this book: Desmond Tutu, Desmond Doss, Desmond Dekker, Desmond Howard, Desmond Meade, Desmond de Silva and Desmond Ball.

Desmond Tutu was a South African hero who helped change his country. He was born in 1931, a sickly little boy from a poor family. As a child, he had polio, which left his right hand permanently deformed. He was also hospitalized for serious burns when he was little.

South Africa was segregated when Desmond Tutu was born. You probably have seen pictures of segregation. Black people were not allowed to use the same public spaces as White people and the best seats were always reserved for White people. It wasn't fair!

Despite these setbacks, Desmond Tutu had a happy childhood. He made toys from scraps and enjoyed playing rugby. He did well in school and especially liked reading.

When he was a boy, he had an experience that deeply moved him. He saw a White man show respect to a Black woman. A priest named Trevor Huddleston tipped his hat to Desmond Tutu's mother while passing them in the street. This simple gesture left him optimistic that Christian faith could help end discrimination. The priest, Trevor Huddleston, was a social activist who later became a mentor to him. He may have been the most influential person in Desmond Tutu's life.

Before Desmond Tutu graduated from high school, things got worse for Black people in South Africa. A policy of apartheid was put in place, which made segregation laws much stricter. Apartheid was a situation where a White minority ruled over a Black majority. Despite this, he was accepted into medical school but couldn't afford the tuition. So, he went to college to become a teacher.

After he graduated and began teaching, he married and had four children. Desmond Tutu taught in an underfunded, overcrowded classroom where a new law was passed to make sure Black South Africans were only educated enough to become servants. After a few years of this, he became frustrated and quit.

Instead, he pursued a dream to become a priest. In 1975 he became the first Black Anglican Dean of Johannesburg, gaining worldwide recognition. He later became the first Black Archbishop of Capetown and used his position to bring about change.

He followed in the footsteps of other world leaders like Gandhi and Martin Luther King, Jr. using civil disobedience. That means he encouraged other South Africans to disobey unfair laws, but never to use violence. Together, Black and White South Africans peacefully disobeyed the unjust laws to bring down apartheid. It was a long struggle, and his strategy was unpopular with others who wanted to violently overthrow the government.

During these hard years, he remembers, "I never doubted that ultimately we were going to be free, because ultimately I knew there was no way in which a lie could prevail over the truth, darkness over light, death over life."

Desmond Tutu won the Nobel Peace Prize for his efforts in 1984, and years later apartheid finally ended in South Africa. It was Desmond Tutu, as the archbishop, who had the honor of introducing his friend Nelson Mandela as the first Black President of South Africa in 1994.

After apartheid ended, Desmond Tutu was chosen to lead the Truth and Reconciliation Commission. Through this, he helped South Africans come to terms with their painful history. In this position he led investigations of wrongdoings and documented them. Those who had wronged others confessed and apologized. In some cases, they paid victims for damages done. He also encouraged the victims to forgive those who had mistreated them. By doing this, Desmond Tutu united South Africans and taught a lesson to the world on reconciliation.

Desmond Tutu said, "Do your little bit of good where you are; it's those little bits of good put together that overwhelm the world." So do your part by doing good for others and you can be part of overwhelming the world, just like Desmond Tutu!

Desmond Doss was an unlikely American war hero. Born in 1919 in Virginia, he was the middle child of his mother and World War I veteran father. His parents raised him in the Seventh-day Adventist faith. That means he was a Christian who followed special rules about what he ate, when he worshipped, and he believed in nonviolence.

Desmond Doss's father suffered from a condition now called PTSD, or post-traumatic stress disorder. That means he had a mental disorder that came from bad memories of wartime. Sadly, his father was sometimes violent, which moved young Desmond Doss to vow to never use a gun.

In 1929, many Americans became poor very suddenly, and Desmond Doss's family struggled to make ends meet. When he finished eighth grade, he got a job at a lumber yard to support his family. Years later, Desmond Doss was working in a shipyard when Japan attacked Pearl Harbor, drawing the United States into World War II.

Because of his job, Desmond Doss could have requested a deferment - that is, an excuse to not be drafted for active duty. Instead, he bravely volunteered for the Army, but refused to kill an enemy soldier or carry a weapon. Because of his beliefs, he was called a conscientious objector. But Desmond Doss considered himself to be a conscientious cooperator, eager to help in any way except for fighting in battle.

At first, Desmond Doss's fellow soldiers and superiors did not think of him as the hero that he was. They were unkind to him and tried to kick him out of the military. But Desmond Doss proved all of them wrong! His comrades began to realize his worth when he healed the blisters on their feet, offered them his own canteen when they were thirsty, and never held a grudge for the awful way that they had treated him. His forgiving attitude took great strength.

Desmond Doss bravely served as a medic during battles in Guam and the Philippines. His bravest moments were during the Battle of Okinawa, when he saved many wounded men in the heat of battle. The battlefield was on top of a huge cliff, surrounded by Japanese machine guns and traps. It looked like the United States would surely lose the battle. When ordered to retreat, Desmond Doss refused to leave his wounded comrades behind. Under enemy fire, he ran alone into the most dangerous zones, carrying wounded soldiers to the edge of the cliff and lowered them all by himself to safety.

Every time he saved a comrade, Desmond Doss prayed aloud, "Lord, please help me get one more." By the end of the night, he had saved about 75 men and was wounded four times in the process! President Harry Truman gave Desmond Doss the Medal of Honor for his bravery, and he became the first conscientious objector to receive this award.

As he pinned on the medal, President Truman said to him, "I consider this a greater honor than being President." After the war, Desmond Doss married and had one son. He gladly talked to people about his wartime experiences and inspired many through his stories! Desmond Doss lived to a ripe old age and always remained anchored in his faith in God.

Desmond Doss teaches us an important lesson about courage and kindness. Be courageous and kind like Desmond Doss!

Desmond Dekker was the first world-famous ska and reggae singer. He was born in 1941 in Jamaica. As a little boy, he attended church and loved to sing hymns. When he grew up, he became a welder and worked in a shop alongside the future reggae legend, Bob Marley. While they worked fusing materials together, they sang. Bob Marley and some other co-workers noticed Desmond Dekker's talent and encouraged him to make his career in music.

It took several auditions and several years, but Desmond Dekker released his first record and became popular in Jamaica. Later, he formed a band with back-up singers and became known as Desmond Dekker and the Aces. They wrote songs about social issues in their culture like the need for children to be educated. Some of their songs had religious themes from the Bible.

In these songs, Desmond Dekker encouraged people not to give up because he believed things would get better. His positive messages and danceable vibes made him popular worldwide. He released more records that became Billboard hits in the United States and England in 1968. Desmond Dekker became the first artist to have a world-famous record that had a uniquely Jamaican sound.

He moved to England the next year and became friends with the members of the Rock N' Roll band, the Beatles. The Beatles wrote and sang a song "Oh Bla Di" about a fictional couple named Desmond and Molly Jones. But Paul McCartney explained that the name Desmond was an artistic nod to his friend Desmond Dekker.

Desmond Dekker paved the way for Jamaican music to take a place on the world stage! The next time you hear reggae music that makes you want to dance, think about talented Desmond Dekker!

Desmond Howard is a former NFL player and a current radio analyst for college football. That means he's an expert, and people like to hear his thoughts about what is going on during the games.

Desmond Howard was born in 1970 in Ohio. He loved football as a little boy, and he was a star football player in high school. He played football at the University of Michigan, where he won the Heisman Trophy. He also received the honor of being voted into the College Football Hall of Fame!

He graduated from college and was the first-round draft pick of the Washington Redskins (now called the Washington Commanders) in 1992. Being the first-round draft pick meant that the team wanted Desmond Howard over any other new player that year. He began a successful football career as a punt and kickoff returner. Later, he played the position of wide receiver.

Throughout his career, Desmond Howard was traded to different teams. His best year was 1996, when he played for the Green Bay Packers. They went to the Super Bowl that year and Desmond Howard won the Super Bowl Most Valuable Player award!

He retired from playing football and now enjoys his current job talking about college football on ESPN. The next time you throw a football, strike a Heisman pose and think about Desmond Howard!

Desmond Meade is a voting rights activist who played an important role in getting a voting law to pass in Florida. He was born in 1967 and grew up in Miami. After he graduated from high school, he joined the United States Army. While serving he was caught stealing, and he was dismissed from the military.

When he returned to Miami, Desmond Meade made more bad choices and became addicted to drugs. On a downward spiral, he got involved in drug-related crimes and was sentenced to 15 years in prison for a felony. A felony is a crime serious enough to be punished by over one year in prison. He was released after three years, based on good behavior.

Upon being released from prison, Desmond Meade found himself homeless in Miami. He realized that he needed to make some drastic changes to turn his life around. So, he completed a drug treatment program and attended college, graduating with straight A's! Then he attended law school and graduated in 2014.

Rather than being bitter about his bad decisions and experiences, Desmond Meade said, "I realized all the pain and suffering I went through all my life became worthwhile when I used it to help someone else."

He became the director of a wonderful program which aims to solve deeper issues related to violence in cities across the United States. Desmond Meade became a hero! In the meantime, he married and now has five children.

Although Desmond Meade became a wonderful example of redemption, Florida law stated that no one who was ever convicted of a felony could vote in elections. So, he worked to change that! He proposed a law where people convicted of felonies could vote if they had first paid their debt to society. In Florida's 2018 election, most people voted in agreement with Desmond Meade, and the bill became law. Because of his great influence, *Time Magazine* honored him by naming him one of the Top 100 people of 2018!

We learn from Desmond Meade to not let our mistakes define us. If you have made some mistakes and think it's too late to turn it around, think again! You can become a hero like Desmond Meade!

Desmond de Silva was a singer known as the "King of Baila." He was born in Sri Lanka in 1944 and began his career in 1963 as the lead singer of a band called the Fireflies. For almost 20 years, he sang with different bands, and was popular on South Asian radio stations.

In 1984, he decided to make a change and sing solo instead. Desmond de Silva was unique for the way he blended different cultures into his Baila music, which has roots in Spain and Portugal. For over 40 years, Desmond de Silva had a successful singing career, packing out concert halls around the world. And his story doesn't stop with his amazing career in music!

In 2005, Desmond de Silva learned about the struggle of many autistic children in Sri Lanka who didn't have the help they needed. Autism is a disorder that makes people have difficulty having social interactions with others. During a concert, Desmond de Silva explained that people with autism think differently and encouraged his fellow Sri Lankans to speak for those who cannot speak for themselves. He made history when he made this speech!

Desmond de Silva was praised by newspapers for having a heart of gold and reaching out to people with autism. If you know anyone with autism, try seeing them with compassion, just as Desmond de Silva did.

Desmond "Des" Ball was an Australian author and intellectual who helped save the world! He was born in 1947 in Nyah West, Australia. When he was born, World War II had just ended, and a different kind of war was just beginning. Two global superpowers, the United States and the Soviet Union, built up nuclear weapons in a decades-long conflict known as the Cold War. During this time, the world was brought to the edge of destruction because the nuclear weapons were powerful enough to blow up the entire planet.

Des Ball was a smart kid who earned a scholarship to attend Australian National University at 17. While in school, he published several books dealing with national security. Looking at the landscape of Australia, he created a plan for defending his country in case of invasion during wartime. He gained a lot of respect since he had a solid plan for defense strategies. At the same time, he believed in keeping peace as much as possible, and thought that building up nuclear weapons was dangerous. Des Ball graduated with a Ph.D. in security studies in 1972.

He spent several months in the United States at the Institute of War and Peace. There, Des Ball was asked to give his opinion about secret plans the United States had to strike and destroy several Soviet targets. After carefully studying the situation, Des Ball shared his opinion that the attack would not work. Instead, he told the officials that their plan would backfire and lead to an all-out nuclear war. Thankfully, the United States officials followed his good advice to not go through with the strike.

Later, the United States President Jimmy Carter recognized his huge contribution in avoiding nuclear war. Des Ball continued his work, helping in the long process of making treaties between the two global superpowers. The treaties worked; the Soviet Union and the United States began to rid the world of nuclear weapons. Finally, in 1991 the Soviet Union collapsed, and the Cold War ended. But Des Ball didn't stop working! He turned his efforts to peacemaking in Southeast Asia.

When we think about people who save the world, we usually think about make-believe characters with superpowers. But Des Ball is a real-life example of a man who helped saved the world! Be a peacemaker and you can be like heroic Des Ball!

This page is all about you!

_____ was born on

_____

As a baby, Desmond _____

_____

As a little boy, Desmond _____

_____

Desmond is especially good at _____

_____

Desmond is often described as _____

_____

Desmond makes people laugh when he _____

_____

One day Desmond would like to _____

_____

This page is for making a self-portrait. A self-portrait is a picture of you, drawn by you!

Bibliography

Abrams, Stacey. "Desmond Meade." *Time100*. time.com. Web. 30 Jun. 2019.

Alzfan, Brittany. "From Felon to Lawyer: The Inspiring Story of Desmond Meade." *Law Street*. lawstreetmedia.com. 9 Jun. 2014.

Bolies, Corbin. "Desmond Meade Spent Three Years in Prison—Now He Wants His Voting Rights Back." *The Reporter*. Mdcthereporter.com. 12 Oct. 2018. Web. 12 Jul. 2019.

"Desmond Dekker Biography." *The biography.com* website. A&E Television Networks. 12 May 2016. Web. 28 Jun. 2018.

"Desmond Doss: The Real Story." *desmonddoss.com* Desmond Doss Council, 2016. Web. 28 Jun. 2018.

"Desmond's Story." *Second Chances*. secondchancesfl.org. Web. 11 Jul. 2019.

"Desmond Tutu Biography." *The biography.com* website. A&E Television Networks. 23 Feb 2018. Web. 28 Jun. 2018.

Farrelly, Nicholas. "Professor Des Ball: The insurgent intellectual." *The Sydney Morning Herald*. smh.com.au. 7 Nov. 2016. Web. 12 Aug. 2019.

Monk, Paul. "Desmond Ball: 1947-2016." *The Interpreter*. lowyinterpreter.org. 14 Oct. 2016. Web. 12 Aug. 2019.

Wikipedia contributors. "Desmond (name)." *Wikipedia, The Free Encyclopedia*. Wikipedia, The Free Encyclopedia, 26 Jun. 2018. Web. 28 Jun. 2018.

Wikipedia contributors. "Des Ball." *Wikipedia, The Free Encyclopedia*. Wikipedia, The Free Encyclopedia, 17 May. 2019. Web. 12 Aug. 2019.

Wikipedia contributors. "Desmond de Silva." *Wikipedia, The Free Encyclopedia*. Wikipedia, The Free Encyclopedia, 26 Mar. 2018. Web. 25 Jun. 2018.

Wikipedia contributors. "Desmond Dekker." *Wikipedia, The Free Encyclopedia*. Wikipedia, The Free Encyclopedia, 3 Apr. 2018. Web. 28 Jun. 2018.

Wikipedia contributors. "Desmond Doss." *Wikipedia, The Free Encyclopedia*. Wikipedia, The Free Encyclopedia, 12 Jun. 2018. Web. 28 Jun. 2018.

Wikipedia contributors. "Desmond Howard." *Wikipedia, The Free Encyclopedia*. Wikipedia, The Free Encyclopedia, 15 Jun. 2018. Web. 18 Jun. 2018.

Wikipedia contributors. "Desmond Tutu." *Wikipedia, The Free Encyclopedia*. Wikipedia, The Free Encyclopedia, 27 Jun. 2018. Web. 28 Jun. 2018.

www.ingramcontent.com/pod-product-compliance
Lightning Source LLC
Chambersburg PA
CBHW042111040426
42448CB00002B/220